ALASTAIR CAMPBE, Yorkshire, in 1957, the son of a vet. After graduating from Cambridge University with a degree in modern languages, his first chosen career was journalism, principally with the Mirror Group. Campbell worked for Tony Blair – first as press secretary, then as official spokesman and director of communications and strategy – from 1994 to 2003, since when he has been mainly engaged in writing, public speaking, consultancy and charity work. He returned to help Labour in the 2005 and 2010 elections. He is an ambassador for the Time to Change campaign to break down stigma and taboo surrounding mental illness. His interests include running, cycling, playing the bagpipes and following the varying fortunes of Burnley Football Club.

Also by Alastair Campbell

Non-fiction

The Blair Years

Diaries Volume One: Prelude to Power

Diaries Volume Two: Power and the People

Diaries Volume Three: Power and Responsibility

Fiction

All in the Mind

Maya

ALASTAIR CAMPBELL

The Happy Depressive

In Pursuit of Personal
and Political Happiness

arrow books

Published by Arrow 2012

11

ISBN 9780099579823

First published in Great Britain in 2012 by Cornerstone Digital

Arrow Books
Random House, 20 Vauxhall Bridge Road,
London SW1V 2SA

www.randomhouse.co.uk

Addresses for companies with The Random House Group Limited can
be found at: www.randomhouse.co.uk

The Random House Group Limited Reg. No. 954009

Typeset by Palimpsest Book Production Limited, Falkirk, Stirlingshire

Penguin Random House is committed to a sustainable future for
our business, our readers and our planet. This book is made from
Forest Stewardship Council® certified paper.

Printed and bound in Great Britain by Clays Ltd, St Ives plc

Welcome to *The Happy Depressive*. That's me. And this is my take on happiness. Friends have suggested that I am the least qualified person to talk about it, because I am often down, and sometimes profoundly depressed. But I think that's where my qualification comes from. Because to know happiness, it helps to know unhappiness. And to me happiness comes from a sense of fulfilment over time, a sense of belonging, relationships which endure, experiences which teach lasting lessons. So I can be grumpy and grouchy, and I can also be depressed. But I'm happy, and the happiness is all the more intense for knowing what it's like to be utterly miserable. It may seem obvious, but I hadn't really worked it out until a man called Thomas Baggs came into my life. I've never met him, and never will. He's dead. Indeed, I had never heard of him until last year when I was asked to deliver the Thomas Baggs Memorial Lecture.

HAPPY, ME?

Thomas Baggs was a graduate of Birmingham University who went on to have a varied career as a teacher, war correspondent and advertising executive, both in the UK and the US. Perhaps imbued with a sense of how they do things in America, when he died aged eighty-four in 1973 it emerged from his will that he had left a generous US-style bequest to his old university. He attached conditions, however. He wanted the money used to fund an annual lecture in his name 'on the subject of happiness – what it is, and how it can be achieved by individuals as well as nations'. These things always being a little more complicated than they sound, it was three years later, in 1976, before the first Thomas Baggs Memorial Lecture was delivered, by Yehudi Menuhin. There has been one every year since, and it has become a familiar date in the calendar for the university, the local community – more than a thousand people attend these events – and that growing band of people who study what it is to be happy, and how we can all do more to deliver happiness. Unsurprisingly, for the Twitter generation, the long title he laid down in his bequest has been shortened to the 'Happiness Lecture', and to my surprise I was asked to deliver it last year.

I was not alone in my astonishment. On telling my daughter, she said, 'Yeah, right.' Fellow Labour strategist Philip Gould, my closest friend, and the one whom I tended to bounce ideas and proposals off when I was unsure of my own views right up until his death last November, just laughed out loud. He was the one who described going on holiday with me and my partner Fiona as being a bit like a series of day trips with the Glums. Fiona, who knows my state of mind better than most, wondered aloud if they had made a mistake, and gone for the wrong Alastair Campbell – I occasionally get confused with Zimbabwe's former cricket captain (though he spells his first name Alistair, not Alastair). In Scotland in particular, it is a fairly common name. I was once approached by a Scot at Euston station, who said, 'You're Alastair Campbell, aren't you?' I said I was. He said, 'My name's Alastair Campbell too.' I smiled and nodded. He added, 'Do you have any idea what my life has been like since you came along?' He didn't seem happy.

Despite the scepticism felt by myself and my nearest and dearest, I committed to do the event, and followed in the footsteps of Denis Healey, David Attenborough, Peter Ustinov, Maureen Lipman, Jonathan Miller and Robert Winston. Even the archetypal grumpy old man Richard Wilson, Victor Meldrew himself, had given his views on happiness.

I was intrigued by the event, and by the subject, and by what I might discover in preparing for it. I write a lot of speeches, these days more for myself than for others, though not exclusively. Often, they can be something of a chore, and even if the financial rewards can be considerable – the private sector speaking market is a fairly large one – the reward for the soul is rarely as great as that provided by a hard day's work. I once found myself blurting out at a speaking gig that professional public speaking was a 'lucrative way of pretending you're still important'.

There was a gap of several months between agreement to speak, and the delivery of the speech. Typically, I didn't get down to writing anything until the event was a week or so away, but in the interim, I found myself asking people, strangers and friends alike, 'What makes you happy?' This was usually met with one of two immediate responses. Response one was a thin smile, which would then broaden. Response two was a confused and worried grimace. I learned over time that the smilers were people who had considered the question before, and lived their lives at least partly in the direct pursuit of happiness, or were at least in possession of an insight that the pursuit of happiness was one of life's purposes. Those who wore the confused and worried look were reacting – and indeed some articulated it exactly in this way – as though they 'never really thought about it'. When I was first approached by the university, my first reaction was the confused and worried look, followed by the thin smile on realising the irony, then a laugh as I sensed this could actually be interesting, a bit different – and 'a bit different' can at least open the door to one of the routes to happiness as I define it below.

AM I HAPPY?

I've certainly realised that in my day-to-day life, I think very little about happiness. That is not to say I don't think about feelings. I probably think about them too much. I brood. I can be introspective. I can also spend too much time worrying about the feelings of others, wishing I could change them when deep down I know that only they can. But when looking at my own feelings, as someone who struggles with depression from time to time, I am more likely to split my assessments of my state of being into 'bad days' and 'not so bad days'. If you have known the depth of a bad day on the depression front, it seems an easier split than 'happy days' and 'unhappy days'. A bad day is one where the mood on waking is rather dark, the feeling in the stomach empty – an emptiness that is not filled by eating – and the effort required to do simple things or make simple decisions is all out of proportion to that required on 'not so bad days'. I have had many 'not so bad days' that I couldn't remotely describe as 'happy'. I have had days I would describe as 'happy' which nonetheless began with this mind-numbing pain and negativity, and the happiness comes only from the sense of the pain lifting, when life recovers an equilibrium of sorts, and the future suddenly looks OK again.

Of course, the obvious approach to the speech – and I think the desire of the university – was for me to talk very personally about my own 'issues', my depression, my drink problem, and the psychotic episode I had in 1986 which brought these issues to the fore. The day of my breakdown was the worst day of my life, yet also the best day of my life. It was the worst at the time, because the insides of my head were literally exploding and in my madness I was convinced I was about to die; the best in retrospect because as a result I confronted a few realities: I had to stop drinking, I had to face up to my depression, and I had to sort out my priorities which essentially meant key relationships, work and politics.

A STATE OF HAPPINESS

By asking the question 'Am I happy?', and via the answer setting out what I mean by happiness, there is a political route that can be taken, by asking another question – 'Can politics deliver happiness, and should it try?' Mr Baggs, after all, had stipulated that the lectures in his memory should look at 'happiness – what it is, and how it can be achieved by individuals *as well as nations*'. He lived perhaps in a less selfish world than we do now, and one where people had a greater readiness to believe in the power of the state to deliver change for the better.

He would identify with the modern politicians who ask whether politics has a role, even a responsibility, to think about happiness when putting together the policies which they run for office on, and eventually govern with.

It is a question that, among others, the prime minister David Cameron has been asking. When analysing policy proposals, UK government ministers have for some years been asked to take account of any economic, social or environmental impact, as well as the effect on gender and racial equality. Now Mr Cameron has added happiness, or general wellbeing, to the factors that policymakers should include when developing policy. 'It is about changing the lens through which we look at policy and its impact,' is how one of the prime minister's advisers on the wellbeing agenda puts it.

It is not easy to see how this would be applied in practice. Economic, social and environmental factors, though they will always be subject to debate and disagreement, are fields at least replete with a mass of statistical analysis based on a near scientific assessment of how a policy actually plays out, and countries can learn from each other as those assessments are made. Happiness is a much more subjective issue, which does not lend itself to similar assessment, beyond perhaps quantitative and qualitative polling. It is nonetheless worth persevering with. There is much I disagree with David Cameron about. I think some of his policies will directly cause unhappiness among some of his electorate. But the idea that happiness should at least be considered when putting forward a policy proposal is a good one. It does not mean that governments can make people happy in the way that families and communities can, but they should think about creating the conditions to do so. About halfway through Tony Blair's premiership, his policy advisers tried to interest him in this agenda, presenting him with a paper, 'Life satisfaction and its policy implications'. He didn't really go for it. It is Cameron who is taking up some of the ideas presented to the predecessor on whom he sometimes models himself.

There is a certain amount of courage required to adopt this approach right now, against the current political backdrop of economic turmoil, austerity, cuts and riots. Unsurprisingly, some within Whitehall are a little nervous at the idea of laying themselves open to analysis by the Office of National Statistics as to how 'happy' we are as a nation. It is bad enough having to pump out information about economic stagnation, rising waiting lists, falling numbers in universities. There is a risk, too, that the government will have to take some of the political rap for what most traditional Conservatives think are issues for families and individuals. To that extent, there is something profoundly non-Conservative at the heart of what Cameron is proposing. He has called the improving of our society's sense of wellbeing 'the central political challenge of our time'.[1] Fond as he is of saying that whatever he happens to be talking about is a top priority, or a central issue, or a challenge that cannot be ducked, there will be scepticism about his commitment to see this through, but I hope he is serious about delivering on the wellbeing agenda.

I hope too that the outcome of his venture is better than that which greeted the fictional British prime minister of Michael Frayn's novel, *A Landing on the Sun*. The PM wanted to explore what government could do to make people happy. His adviser on the subject went mad in the process, and met the ultimate unhappy ending – death. I do not wish such a fate upon Mr Cameron or his team.

I wish him all the best with a Civil Service machine that is not always quick to adapt to new thinking, and which in any event he is cutting to the bone. I wish him all the best with ministers who will probably snort that they did not come into politics 'to make people happy'. Indeed, there are signs that senior civil servants are taking to this new approach with greater enthusiasm than Cameron's colleagues around the Cabinet table. Shortly before he stepped down last December, Cabinet Secretary Sir Gus O'Donnell wrote to Permanent Secretaries in all government departments telling them the prime minister meant business on this.

It is not an easy issue, and coordination of cultural change across government not an easy task. If Cameron is serious about making this a significant change of approach, he will need to use up a fair amount of his leadership tokens. He made the first steps down this path in relatively good times, as he was rising to the top of British politics. But he has to implement the change in what could turn out to be persistently bad times. Yet what he said when he first broached this issue is as true today as it was back in 2006, perhaps even more so. 'It's time we admitted that there's more to life than money and it's time we focused not just on GDP but on GWB – general wellbeing ... Wellbeing can't be measured by money or traded in markets. It's about the beauty of our surroundings, the quality of our culture and, above all, the strength of our relationships.'[2]

Cameron is not alone in exploring the happiness route. A UN summit on the theme of wellbeing is planned for this spring. Canada's government is taking a similar approach to that of the UK. EU President Herman Van Rompuy is also on the happiness agenda. The week before Christmas last year, and at the end of an extremely turbulent year for the Eurozone in particular and the world economy in general – he made a point of sending to 200 global leaders a copy of *The World Book of Happiness*, a collection of essays about happiness, with the message: 'My request to you as world leaders is to make people's happiness and wellbeing our political priority for 2012.'

President Nicolas Sarkozy of France has also stated that happiness and wellbeing should be included in any measurement of economic success.[3] He has taken a close interest in the work of Joseph Stiglitz and Amartya Sen, Nobel Prize-winning economists who have been urging a shift from a purely economic analysis of a country's success or relative failure, to one which includes and is even dominated by an analysis of wellbeing and sustainability. Sarkozy wants to know how much time French people sit in traffic jams, whether they feel they can improve their work–life balance, whether women feel equal in the workplace. All, he believes, can have an impact on people's sense of wellbeing, as individuals and communities. There is a heavy emphasis on the environment in the Stiglitz–Sen findings, their view being that a country which grows sustainably is likely to be happier than one which damages its own environment. They also emphasise the importance of seeing economic figures in the context of household wealth, not the big numbers regularly proclaimed by ministers, economists and analysts.[4] Ministers, though, should perhaps be worried about the evidence in economic statistics of a growing gap between rich and poor, because the empirical evidence in happiness research suggests it is not so much the actual lack of wealth of the individual that delivers unhappiness, but the feeling that he or she is not getting a fair share, and feels remote from and envious of the people doing so much better.

Mr Cameron seems undeterred by all that, and last year the independent national statistician Jil Matheson was commissioned to devise a set of questions that would be included in the next household survey, a key tool in policymaking in that it tries to establish what kind of lives people are living. Her independence was emphasised when the initiative was announced, but what the government hoped for was for people to be polled at regular intervals on their sense of wellbeing. Four questions were added to the survey to assess people's sense of personal wellbeing, both generally and how they have felt in recent days, and to assess how worthwhile they consider their lives to be. Two hundred thousand people are covered by the current survey and the full responses are expected to be published in the spring, including local breakdowns so that we can learn which parts of the country are 'happiest'. A taster, published in December, which covered just over 1,100 adults, suggested that around three-quarters of British people were currently satisfied with their lives. But a sample as large as two hundred thousand will have a far greater value for public and policy-makers alike.

If the exercise works, and it takes hold within government and with the public, then the 'happiness stats' could become a regular in the calendar, like crime figures, growth figures and educational results. More importantly, perhaps, if the stats become embedded as part of the governmental and political cycle, then over time they can begin to have a real impact on policy decisions. The Canadians are ahead of the UK in the polling analysis of their citizens' assessment of their own wellbeing, but even the people in charge of that polling say the UK will be ahead of all developed economies if the government uses the data it gathers actively to influence public policy. In addition, the mere existence of such a huge survey and its results will affect the population's decisions on where they choose to work, live and bring up their families.

MONEY CAN'T BUY ME LOVE

David Cameron would no doubt argue that the country cannot be happy unless there are strong economic foundations. He would argue that those cannot be built without reducing the deficit and therefore making major cuts to public services. Someone analysing the role of Educational Maintenance Allowances in extending opportunities to poorer children would easily find plenty of recipients who, even if they would not have described themselves as 'happy' to have been in receipt of it, will certainly say they are 'unhappy' to be losing it. In schools which were expecting funds from the Building Schools for the Future programme, which the government ended, teachers, governors and students were far from happy about its demise. Similarly, students who felt able to access university at lower fees and with lower debt levels than those now being proposed will not be happy to find their opportunities now diminished.

Assuming the happiness debate was already live when these decisions were made, Cameron and Chancellor George Osborne will have decided that the greater good required them to make them. It leaves a lot of unhappy people dealing with the consequences, but sometimes in politics that is inevitable. This is one of the great political truths: governments make choices that cannot make all of the people happy all of the time. That much I accept. What would be unfortunate is if in fact Cameron's commitment to happiness as a key factor in policymaking was something he just said at the time he was busy 'decontaminating' the Conservative brand – one of his early strategic goals in opposition – rather than a change of culture he is determined to implement, because I do think if we genuinely applied this new approach it could lead to a lot of positive change.

Our approach to the economy under both Labour and Tory governments, and now with the coalition, and indeed governments around the world, is to focus on GDP. It explains why something verging on panic – the polite code words are 'crisis of confidence' – materialises whenever poor economic stats combine with a plunge in the over-mighty markets. Although we have grown much wealthier as a country and, most of us, as individuals, we are not happier. The Labour peer Professor Richard Layard, who can perhaps lay claim to being the first 'happiness economist' in British policymaking, made a big impact on me when I saw a presentation in which he superimposed two graphs – one for our personal wealth which showed a steady rise, and one for our happiness which showed a flatline ending with a bit of a dip. The Canadian government's research showed greater unhappiness in the country's richer provinces than the poorer ones.

A driving focus on personal wealth creation may well bring material gain, but it is in our relationships with others and within communities that we will find happiness. People who become wealthy adapt quickly to their new wealth, which becomes every bit as 'normal' as the circumstances they left behind. Look at how readily young working-class boys can become multimillionaire footballers within a matter of years, and behave as if to the manor born, or how bankers can move from relatively low salaries to multimillion bonuses early in their careers, and find themselves not that much happier, but more envious of the footballer or the banker who has even more. As I argued above, our actual wealth appears to be less important to us than the comparisons we make with others,

HAPPINESS IN THE UK VS. GDP PER CAPITA

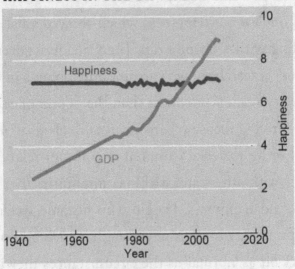

Source World Database of Happiness + Penn Tables.

not just with regards to wealth, but status too. However, there can only be one 'richest man in the world' – Mr Carlos Slim as things stand – and he probably wishes he was the Queen. And when two of Russia's wealthiest oligarchs, Roman Abramovich and Boris Berezovsky, clashed in a London court recently, I couldn't help noticing how utterly miserable they both looked.

But there I am falling into a trap Professor Layard

warns us against. He made the point that when governments assess happiness they do so based on their *judgement* of how people would feel rather than on any rigorous assessment of how people *actually* feel. So it will be interesting to see how Cameron assesses the change as he tries to steer it through a wary system. He starts with Britain not faring brilliantly. Under work commissioned by the Government Office for Science on behalf of the last government, the New Economics Foundation measured personal and social wellbeing in twenty-two European countries.[5] Denmark came top. In the UK older people scored highly, but young people had the lowest levels of trust and sense of belonging anywhere in Europe. In 2009, a survey carried out by York University, on behalf of the Child Poverty Action Group, concluded that British children were the least happy of any wealthy European country.[6] Though I don't do God, I found myself nodding along with the Archbishop of Canterbury, Rowan Williams, when he said, 'The selling of lifestyles to children creates a culture of material competitiveness and promotes acquisitive individualism at the expense of the principles of community and cooperation.'[7] Amen to that.

Can anyone really dispute that as families have struggled to stay together, as communities have fractured, so trust between people has eroded, relationships have weakened, and we have grown less happy as a result? The focus on extreme individualism has not in the main made for happier individuals. And millions of unhappy individuals make for an unhappy nation, and unhappy nations make for an unhappy world.

If that sounds too simplistic, then I make no apology for it. In the US, trust in other people being 'nice' has fallen from 60 per cent to 30 per cent in fifty years. It is the same story in the UK. In 1959, 60 per cent of people felt other people could generally be trusted. It has now halved. Layard believes that decline has matched the rise

INCOME AND HAPPINESS IN THE UNITED STATES

of consumerism which has been accompanied by a rise in the obsession with status, and envy of those who do better than us.[8]

Though wealth does not automatically confer happiness upon those who have it – indeed some of the least happy people I know are among the richest – there is a clearer link between poverty and *un*happiness. Professor Gary Cooper led an interesting study for the New Economics Foundation, in which he took a cradle-to-grave look at scientifically proven causes of mental ill health.

I am not equating all unhappiness with mental illness, but it is worth looking at what he found. Some people are born mentally ill. Others are born with a likely genetic disposition to mental illness. But what Professor Cooper did was set out factors that are not dependent on birth, but on background and upbringing: economic, social and personal circumstances.

To look at just a few is to show how close the overlap may be between areas of personal responsibility and a role for the government, or at least an acceptance of responsibility that it may well be able to influence those factors which cause greater unhappiness and mental illness. Poor housing. Poor diet. Lack of parental attention as a child. Poor parenting skills. Debt. Bullying. Poor education. Learning difficulties. Crime. Unemployment. Stigma and discrimination. Isolation. Drugs. Alcohol dependency.

Merely to list those issues is to confirm that government policy is, or at least can and should be, linked directly to general wellbeing. That would certainly seem to be the view of those polled by the New Economics Foundation on the subject. Eighty-one per cent expressed the view that government *should* prioritise creating happiness over creating wealth.[9] The poll was conducted some years ago, at a time when rising prosperity was perhaps taken for granted. But that figure is large enough to suggest it will not have been wholly eroded even by the economic crisis of 2007/8, or the one the world is afraid of right now.

GROSS NATIONAL HAPPINESS

Putting happiness at the heart of policymaking is not a new thing. The tiny Buddhist kingdom of Bhutan has for many years had gross national happiness as its main indicator, though the methodology is seen by some as being slanted in favour of the regime. Spin, Buddhist-style. Yet where once it was all seen by the bigger countries as hopelessly idealistic, perhaps a bit silly, now it would seem the

Bhutanese have been ahead of their time. It was their king, Jigme Khesar Namgyel Wangchuk, who is thought to have first used the phrase 'gross national happiness' as a deliberate contrast to the gross domestic product seen by less spiritual countries as the holy grail. He wanted to put Bhutan's cultural and spiritual values at the heart of their approach to the economy. The Centre for Bhutan Studies, with outside help, developed their own system for measuring wellbeing, based on four 'pillars': the promotion of equitable and sustainable socioeconomic development; the preservation and promotion of traditional cultural values; conservation of the natural environment; and good governance.

Though it is possible to see how those four areas and the approach underpinning them might appeal, especially to a Buddhist, they are not confined to one faith or political system. It is equally possible to see how they relate to the priorities for wellbeing set out by Mr Cameron or President Sarkozy.

Let's sloganise them. Vote for:

a fair economy
a strong culture
a healthy environment
good governance

What leader in the modern world would set his or her face against any of that? But it is in the detailed policies and their impact on society that one can measure whether the principles are being applied, and there it is possible to pick apart the UK or French government approach more easily than when looking at Bhutan, admittedly a much smaller and less complicated country.

It is easy to dismiss the four Bhutanese pillars for their generality, but there is greater specificity, and with it greater pressure on policymakers, through the subsections they name as key contributors to happiness: physical, mental and spiritual health; providing the right balance of time spent on work, leisure and family; strength of communities and social structures; the vitality of local and national culture; education; living standards; good governance; and ecological vitality.

Whether because the idea came from the king, or because they have had more time to develop the approach, the Bhutanese do more than pay lip service to the concept of happiness as a key factor when devising policy. Gross national happiness is seen not just as a unifying national vision, but all economic and social plans are put through a GNH test related to these areas, and have to pass it. It has been compared with the environmental assessment to which US policies are subjected.[10]

The concepts and issues at the heart of the Bhutanese approach are not that dissimilar to the metric used by Med Jones, president of the International Institute of Management, based on a series of statistical measurements and public opinion testing of what he calls economic wellness, environmental wellness, physical wellness, mental wellness, workplace wellness, social wellness and political wellness.[11] Economic wellness includes issues like debt levels (consumer as well as national), fairness of income distribution, the relationship between earnings and prices. Environmental wellness would have at its heart an assessment of pollution, noise, traffic and people's appreciation of their natural surroundings. Mental wellness would be recorded in part by the measurement of drugs used to deal with depression, and the numbers of people using psychological services. Workplace wellness is not just about having a job, but what satisfaction and security people get from it. Social wellness is a question of whether people feel respected and appreciated by others, safe in their communities, strong in their families and relationships. Political wellness is about the quality of democracy, and freedom.

Perhaps Mr Cameron and President Sarkozy will discover that there are certain universal truths attached to what makes people and nations 'happy'. But in research study after research study, the same Bhutanese-style theme comes through, that – to quote a very clever Finnish Burnley supporter, Olli Issakeinen, who makes hugely intelligent comments on my blog – 'unhappiness seems to be the ultimate luxury'.

Nor is this view confined to the north of Europe, where Norwegians are number one in the world table for human development, and the Danes, as I pointed out earlier, number one for happiness, and the Finns have what is seen as the best education system in the world. From the heart of the US establishment, Harvard University Professor of Psychology Daniel Gilbert, author of *Stumbling On Happiness* and known as 'Professor Happiness', published research showing big increases in happiness for people who move step by step towards a middle-class income of between $40,000 and $70,000 (in UK terms between £24,000 and £43,000). But once that level is reached, increases in wealth generate only negligible rises in happiness and wellbeing.[12] So wealth accumulated by and allocated to individuals beyond these amounts reflects money wasted in terms of improving wellbeing and happiness for society as a whole. So here is something David Cameron's right wing will not wish to hear: if we are serious about maximising wellbeing across the whole of society, the research leaves no doubt that the best way would be to close the gap between low and middle incomes as much as possible and for as many people as we can. Equally, where there is a finite amount of money going round a society, allowing increases for the richer few beyond a middle bracket is a waste as it does not proportionally increase happiness and wellbeing to the same extent as would occur allocating the same resources to individuals further down the ladder. I hope David Cameron is serious about this.

Bhutan has practised the approach suggested by such research more than Britain. Unsurprisingly,

Britain's 'Happiness Professor', Richard Layard, has been to Bhutan, and was impressed, not least by their belief, matched by policy, that the redistribution of wealth, if it favours the poor, is likely to add to the happiness of all. Merely to state that is to underline what a challenge Cameron may have in a country where envy – some of it media-driven, some of it real – is directed upwards towards the undeserving rich as represented now by corporate greed and symbolised by the banks, and downwards to so-called benefit cheats and welfare scroungers living off the hard work of others.

A CULTURE OF NEGATIVITY

It is hard to know how much of the envy and loathing in our society is real, and how much a creation of our uniquely negative and negativising media. Before his death, former Foreign Secretary Robin Cook used to quote an academic study which stated that the positive to negative ratio in the UK press had gone from 3:1 in 1974, to 1:18 in the present day. Some years ago, I was at a dinner at the French Embassy in London, and seated next to the Arsenal manager, Arsene Wenger. He said he loved his job, loved living in London, loved English football, the crowds, the passion, the appreciation of the game. The one thing he couldn't understand about Britain, though, was the negativity of the media. But when I suggested he say so publicly, as a respected outsider challenging this culture of negativity, he said something very interesting. 'I'm not sure it is worth it. If it did not speak to something deep in the British public psyche, I don't think the press here would be like it is.' In other words, not only do we get the media we deserve, but we get the media we want. He may well have a point, but I hope not. I do not believe the British people are as negative, as spiteful or as consumed by envy as many of our papers would suggest.

But it is very hard to see how as a country we can be deemed happy when every day more than two million of our people feel the urge to imbibe the poison of the *Daily Mail*. How can we be happy knowing that merely to step out of our Middle England front door is to risk being mugged by feral kids and asylum seekers, and to know that a fair economy, a strong culture, a healthy environment and good governance don't exist, and that economic wellness, environmental wellness, physical wellness, mental wellness, work-place wellness, social wellness and political wellness are for others. Envy, hatred and anger do not lend themselves to happiness. Yet much of our media, most of the time, is now slavishly dedicated to making people feel jealous of others, to blame others for their problems, to hate others for their actions and attitudes. The post-Internet papers have created a kind of whingeocracy in which the issues for moaning about are published each morning, and then the radio and TV stations can moan about them for the next twenty-four hours until the next lot of whinges come round. Add in the criminality we have seen exposed in the phone-hacking scandal recently, its amorality and venality, and it is not a happy scene.

The relentless negativity is a relatively new thing, a lot of it driven by the advent of 24/7 news and the Internet which has forced newspapers to adapt, and to rely more on impact to make a noise in this ever noisier and more competitive marketplace. There came a day when I genuinely ceased to care what the media said about me. It was liberating. It has helped my happiness. When you have been compared not just to Goebbels but to Hitler, there really aren't many other insults left. But the extremity of the insult is born of the addiction to negativity and impact. They feel they have to be negative because (wrongly in my view) they believe that is what sells (they have somehow failed to notice their decline has coincided with the addiction to negativity, and blamed it on technological developments out of their control). And they feel they have to get ever more negative to make the impact. But once you decide that actually it doesn't much matter what they say, and that it is entirely possible to survive and endure enormous amounts of negativity and still remain standing, still do the things you believe in, the feeling of strength and liberation is intensified.

HAPPINESS AND ILL HEALTH

In several of my various capacities – as a depressive, a mental health campaigner, and a Labour activist – I had cause to appreciate Richard Layard's influence on the last government, when in 2005 he made a powerful presentation to the Downing Street Strategy Unit arguing that mental illness had replaced unemployment as Britain's Biggest Social Problem. More mentally ill people were drawing incapacity benefits than there were unemployed people on Jobseeker's Allowance. So depression was not merely bad for gross national happiness. It was bad for GDP too. As many as one in six people suffered from depression or anxiety (I think that may be conservative by the way), yet just a quarter of them were getting any kind of treatment, and usually that meant drugs. In a paper he wrote later, called *The Depression Report*,[13] he recommended training an additional 10,000 clinical psychologists and psychological therapists to provide cognitive behavioural therapy for people suffering from depression and anxiety through 250 local treatment centres, offering courses of therapy costing £750. Each course would pay for itself in money saved on incapacity benefits and lost tax receipts.

It was partly this economic argument that led the government to extend the scope and funding for CBT, and to set up a new programme for the NHS in England, still rolling out despite the change in government, called Improving Access to Psychological Therapies. Here, the mental health campaigns will be keeping a close eye on Cameron and his commitment to an agenda for wellbeing. Historically, when health budgets have been under pressure, the mental health services have tended to go to the back of the queue. There are signs that it is happening again. In my own area of north London, Camden, two of the four centres for emergency treatment of the mentally ill have gone. Part of the argument was that often they were not full. That is partly their purpose – a spare capacity that can be used when needed by a seriously ill individual. In an ideal world, there would be no need for such places at all. But the need is greater, not lesser, when both mental illness and unhappiness are on the rise.

The National Health Service is one of the great civilising achievements of British life and history, but government can only do so much. Set out priorities. Allocate funding. Issue guidelines. When the NHS was founded under Labour's post-war health minister Nye Bevan, his statement that 'when a bedpan falls to the floor in Tredegar Hospital, its sound should echo in the Palace of Westminster' was always more a wonderful piece of rhetoric than it was a system for running healthcare. He was emphasising, at a time of considerable opposition to his plans, that government had a responsibility to deliver good care to all, and to ensure those working for the NHS delivered it. But good health has always been as much the responsibility of the individual as it is of the state, especially so now that there can be few of us unaware of the dangers of smoking, drinking and bad diet, or the benefits of healthy eating and exercise. Insofar as David Cameron's government accepts physical and mental wellness as key challenges, preventative health-care policies require development every bit as much as the more obvious and – to policy wonks at least – more interesting challenges of how to run the hospitals and the health services. The government does the macro. The individual has to do the micro.

IS CONTENTMENT THE SAME AS HAPPINESS?

Again, there is considerable agreement among 'the happiness community' about what the individual should strive to do to maintain wellbeing. The New Economics Foundation brought together research from four hundred scientists around the world and, with 'five a day' for fruit and vegetables fairly well established in the public mind as a guide to healthy eating, came up with a 'five a day' for general wellbeing.[14]

Connect with the people around you

Be active

Take notice – be curious and aware of the world around you

Keep learning – try something new

Give – do something nice for a friend or a stranger

It is interesting that whenever I am going through a depressed phase, I feel less desire to connect with other people, and can become antisocial to the point of reclusiveness, not answering the phone even to friends, not opening mail; I find it harder to generate the enthusiasm and energy required for the strenuous physical exercise that I like to do every day, and which I know is vital to my mental wellbeing; my curiosity and interest in the world around me, let alone a desire to try something new, vanish; and I become less giving as I become more insular and isolated. Equally, if I think of the things that sometimes help lift me from depression, they would certainly include forcing myself to go out and meet people (though sometimes it can make things worse); exercise almost always has a positive effect; forcing myself to read about something I know nothing about or do something I have never done before can also bring immediate benefits – I once found myself slowly emerging from a depression by buying Fiona some flowers and taking them for a run over Hampstead Heath before handing them over with an apology for my miserableness of the past few days. It was in part the ludicrousness of the situation and the laughs and looks of others that lifted me as I ran with this enormous bouquet. Then again, it might have been coincidental. And finally, the point about giving is vital – if I wake up on a depressed day to find a voluntary sector commitment in the diary, I resent it, but I almost invariably feel better afterwards.

Experience has told me that the negative intensity of a bad bout of depression is stronger than the positive intensity of feelings of wellbeing. I may have more of the latter, but for me at least the power of the former is greater. It probably explains why I analysed the 'five a day' from the perspective of depression rather than happiness. I am actually happier far more often than I am depressed. It's just that the 'glad to be alive' feeling is not as gripping, physically and mentally, as the all-enveloping, deadening numbness that comes when the depressive force seems to take over blood, bones and mind.

So is it the Presbyterian (by upbringing) in me, or the Labour man, or the charity worker, or the idealist and optimist, or the depressive, or a mix of all of them, that asks: Are we, in fact, here to be happy? Or might it be that we are here to become better people and make a better world, and only in so doing will we find meaningful happiness?

I can *feel* happy reading a good book – you know that moment a few pages in where you think, yep, this is going to be a good one, and then anything else is just a distraction ... I can feel happy watching a good film or listening to good music ... But am I? Maybe it is less happiness than successful distraction from the reality of the human condition which is not so much permanent happiness or unhappiness as 'let's try to get through the day'?

Stimulation is not the same as happiness. Excitement is not the same as happiness. I'm not even convinced that contentment is the same as happiness, whatever the dictionary may say.

Oddly, given my own state, my mum is one of the happiest people I know. Rarely down, always smiley and singing, rarely a bad word to say and never a bad word said about her.

Yet often she will say to me, 'Why can't you just be *content*?' Well, often I am. It's just not the same thing as happiness. I can be content after a good meal, but still worry about a big project coming up that is making me edgy and nervous. I can be content after a Burnley win but not happy that I am besotted with a football club based four hours from where I live. I enjoy the journey there, hate the journey back. Every second Saturday I do it and win, lose or draw between arrival home and *Match of the Day* something happens and Fiona will say, 'I don't know why you go to Burnley – it never seems to make you *happy*.' It does make me pleased, excited, thrilled, engaged, enervated, often disappointed, but not happy that it takes four hours to get home to a partner who hasn't even bothered to find out the score.

DOES THE WINNER REALLY TAKE IT ALL?

When I think back to happy moments, they are a strange mix, and the ones that people might expect to be there are not. I was closely involved in three election wins. These are big moments not just in my life but more importantly the life of the country. When I transcribed my diaries, I spotted a trend. Let's start with 1997. The scene is Tony Blair's house in Sedgefield and here is my diary entry, late at night after the campaign has finished and the country is about to vote.

TB said afterwards he would never have been able to do it without me. I said I'd loved every minute, then said 'That's a lie by the way.' I called home and spoke to the kids ... I said life is never going to be the same again, because this is part of history and we're all part of that, our whole family. Calum said 'Are we definitely going to win?' I loved the 'we'. I said yes, I think so, and we might win big. After I put the phone down, I sat down on the bed, put my head in my hands and cried my eyes out. I don't know what it was. Relief it was over. Letting go of the nervous energy. Pride. A bit of fear. It was all in there. But I felt we'd done a fantastic job. We were going to win and we were going to make a difference. I'd felt the emotion welling up in me for days ... I'd been worrying about Dad's health and was glad he and Mum would both see this happening, but sad that Bob [Fiona's father], who'd always said one day Labour will get back, wasn't there to see it, or even know that Fiona and I had been involved.

I vividly recall the moment I finally admitted to myself we were going to win. The morning of the vote, campaigning over. I went down to the kitchen in the Sedgefield house, where Tony's agent John Burton was listening to the *Today* programme. I switched to a music channel, and on came Abba, 'The Winner Takes It All'. But does he?

We had won bigger than any of us had ever imagined – we were even winning in seats we had not campaigned in. Here is my diary entry for the Festival Hall:

It was weird. I felt deflated. All around us people were close to delirium but I didn't feel part of it ... We were taken up to a room afterwards, and I said to TB, this is so weird, you've worked so hard for so long for something, it comes, you're surrounded by people who are so happy ... yet you don't feel like they do, and you just want to get home to bed. He said he felt exactly the same.

Four years later, we had won another landslide, and the only moment I felt any joy was when I saw my other son Rory waiting for me at Millbank Tower as we arrived for the victory party, and here is how I close the entry for this, the day of our second great victory.

In some ways, I had enjoyed the night more than in 1997, but I still didn't feel the kind of exhilaration others seemed to. It was also because I knew there would be no let-up, and in all sorts of ways the future was unclear. Maybe it was just my nature.

I am only up to 2001 in the published diaries but here is a sneak preview of 2005, another win, and this extract starts after the victory party in London.

I was now beginning to share TB's sense of disappointment at the result. It was light by the time I left and I got a really nice reception from people as I was walking to Victoria Street. A few people were shouting out congratulations from cars. But I felt a bit low about it all. I said goodbye to a few people at party HQ and as I made for the door, there was a spontaneous round of applause. I stopped and looked back and there was a standing ovation going on, which I found really moving. I felt like these were the people I really loved working with… I felt my eyes filling with tears and must have looked like I was crying when I got into the cab home. 'You should be happy,' the cabbie said. 'Three in a row.'

So what do I make of all that? Well, first, for a man with a hard image, I cry a lot. As Rory said when *The Blair Years* was published, 'Dad, do we really have to have all this crying crap?' Second, I cry when I am happy in the sense of my being fulfilled, job done. Third, it is family that has the capacity to move us most, because they are the people we love most. Fourth, I will always resent the fact that I did not enjoy three of the greatest days of my life. Fifth, other than in sport I find it hard to lose myself in mass emotion – I prefer to stand out against it than go along with it. But, sixth, I never stop thinking about the next thing, and the next thing, and the fears about the challenge ahead will drive my mood every bit as much as any pleasure there may be in the moment.

THE HAPPY DEPRESSIVE

For me happiness is not about moments – though they can build towards it – but about fulfilment over time. I think the pursuit of those things that many people may think make them happy in our consumer society – fame, money, alcohol, drugs, quick-hit relationships – are less likely to make people happy than give them a sense of elation, the endurance of which is all too elusive.

If you ask me if I am happy that I devoted a large part of my life to helping Labour get elected and then helping Tony Blair in government, I will say yes. If you ask me if I was happy all the time doing it, read the books; talk to Fiona and the kids, and understand why they think it is funny that I was asked to talk about happiness.

If fame was the answer, then you wouldn't have the extraordinary situation where 'real people' often seem happier than the famous. I know plenty of both. The famous ones are, in general, more disgruntled than the not so well known who are likely to be more pressurised financially and in numerous other ways. How many stories do you read of the rich and their problems? Or lottery winners who regret the win? The reason for Professor Layard's graph diversion is that we adapt to wealth quickly. We get a bigger salary, or a bigger house, a bigger car, a more expensive holiday; then we sit around saying how much fun we had when we were struggling. And for the really wealthy, there is never enough. As for drugs and alcohol and gambling and the other well-known areas of addiction, nobody can ever tell me that the addict finds happiness in a bottle, a needle or a punt.

So despite being grumpy, despite being a depressive who occasionally needs medication to deal with it, I am reasonably happy. That seems like a bit of a conundrum. It has also given me the title for this book, *The Happy Depressive*. I am both, and sometimes at the same time; because I am reasonably fulfilled, and the fulfilment has not been easy. That's the other thing – to me, any sense of happiness requires a sense of fulfilment and any fulfilment, worthwhile fulfilment, requires struggle. It doesn't come easy.

I know this is not a universal view. Fiona's version of my mum's 'why can't you just be content?' is 'why do you keep needing to do so much?' A variation, which I hear when I wake up groaning because of aching joints from over-exercising, then grunts about how much I have to do in the day ahead is: 'why do you keep torturing yourself?' Her observation of my life patterns is that I decide to do something, throw myself into it, do it well, but then decide I need something else. 'You're never *happy*.' That is not strictly true. I have moments, but the building of happiness through fulfilment is a long game.

So here is my theory of happiness: we cannot know if we have lived a truly happy life until the very end. It's a dark theory, I confess, but then one of Labour's former MPs, Clare Short, did once call me the man who lived in the dark.

THE DEATH AND LIFE OF PHILIP GOULD

This view of life and death has, however, been reinforced by my close witnessing of the build-up to the death of Philip Gould. Philip was without doubt my closest friend in politics, and unusually for an adult friend, adored as much by our children as he was by Fiona and me. When he died, I felt like I had lost a limb. Even now, I find myself texting him for his thoughts on a problem, or simply to tell him something funny I have heard or observed, and am halfway through tapping out the message before remembering: he's not here.

As I said at his funeral, when at his request – one of the last he made before slipping into unconsciousness – I read out a letter I had written to him the day before he died,[15] I will remember him not for his fight against cancer, but for the life force he was during the healthy times. He was a bundle of ideas and energy and positivity whose enthusiasms could excite and inspire me, but at other times – like when I was depressed – drive me a bit crazy. But he was an amazing friend, always there when I needed help and support, and always capable of lifting me even in my lowest moments.

So through a succession of political campaigns, crises, holidays and family dramas, we became as close as the closest of brothers, and the closeness grew during the final months of his terminal illness. I said in my letter that he was there for so many of the happiest moments of our lives, and often the cause of the happiness, as well as always being there in the tough times too. Friendship is fundamental to happiness, and you are never more aware of it than when you lose a friend. Anji Hunter, a friend and colleague to both of us, said to me when Philip was first diagnosed with oesophageal cancer: 'Remind me never to be your best friend.'

The reason was that Philip is not my first close friend to die young. John Merritt, my closest friend in journalism, died aged thirty-five from leukaemia in 1992, and his daughter Ellie died six years later from the same disease. Mark Gault, my flatmate at university, dropped dead of a heart attack in 2003 – in the same week as the BBC report on the so-called 'sexing up' of the WMD dossier which would lead to more death and destruction. And Richard Stott, the *Mirror* editor who had thrown me a lifeline in offering me my old job back when I cracked up after leaving the *Mirror* for *Today* against his wishes, and who later edited my diaries, was another very close friend taken horribly early.

Philip's death was different. He made it an event, a campaign even. Every campaign needs a simple goal, and he had one – survival. He beat the cancer twice, with the help of his own strength and some amazing medical practitioners, with the Brits of the NHS better than the private sector he originally chose in the United States. He used to talk of the fight in the same terms as an election. He had a 'message' for the cancer – 'It can just fuck off.' We had a name for it – Adolf. This meant he was Churchill. He liked that. He had a 'grid' for his hospital visits, the chemo, the pills. He called me shortly after being first diagnosed and said, 'I have had the PET scan.' Not being a medical person, I asked what a PET scan was, to which he replied, 'It is basically the exit poll.'

'Oh,' I said, 'how's it looking?' To which he replied, 'The momentum is with us, but it's all within the margin of error.'

When the cancer came back a second time, he was warned if it came back a third time, he was a goner. When it did, he pursued a twin strategy – fight as hard as he could, but prepare himself and others for his death. He wrote a remarkable account of his illness,[16] and updated his book *The Unfinished Revolution*, about how New Labour changed first the party and then the country. He talked obsessively about all the details, not just of his treatment but of his funeral and what would follow. He insisted we visit his burial plot at Highgate (which he wanted even though he was being cremated). We sat in the autumn sunshine on a nearby bench and he said how much it meant to him that John – 'your best friend before me' – and Ellie were nearby, down by Karl Marx. He said he felt I was changing as a person as a result of his death. I didn't think I was, to be honest, but he was convinced – and happy – that I was.

He said he was happy to know his daughters would have lots of support but he worried more about his wife Gail. He was happy at the intensity of discussions he had had about religion with Tony Blair, about grief with Gordon Brown. It was at times almost as though he was talking about someone else. I said, 'Philip, you can't really be happy you're going to die.' 'Well, no,' he said, 'but I feel I have lived a good life and I feel these days and weeks have been amazing, maybe the most intense days and feelings of my life. It has made me feel whole. It has made me appreciate my life, my politics, my family, my friendships, more than I would if I had gone on and on and died of old age. I really do feel happy about that.'

I developed my theory that we only know if we have lived a happy life as we near its end (which I also mentioned in my letter to him) long before Philip became ill. He used to mock me for it, and see it as part of my characteristic glumness, which was such a contrast to his relentless enthusiasm. But his own experience confirmed it to me. It was at times wonderful to watch him – TV viewers saw a glimpse of it in an interview he did with Andrew Marr on the BBC[17] – being so open and insightful about the process of dying, and the greater clarity it brought to his thinking and his assessment of his life. We also found space for great humour once he was into (his phrase) 'the death zone'.

In the Marr interview, Philip said the doctor had told him he had three months to live. In fact – he often muddled his thoughts and words, just as he often lost laptops, briefcases and pass-ports – the doctor said 'months' and the 'three' just popped into Philip's head and popped out of his mouth. From that day on, we indulged in ever more elaborate fantasy planning of a photo call with Abdelbaset al-Megrahi, the Libyan terrorist released from prison in Scotland in August 2009 on grounds of being terminally ill, and still going strong a long time after. 'How many days to Operation al-Megrahi?' he would ask. In the end, he didn't quite make the three months.

On the same day I suggested to him that the volume of post-death events being planned risked going over the top – 'You're not the Queen Mother,' I said – Carol Linforth of the Labour Party asked me if I thought they should get Philip in before he died and present him with a book of messages from staff and former colleagues. She seemed taken aback when I said, 'Yes, like a giant "Get Dead Soon" card.' But nobody laughed louder than Philip. He brought hope and happiness to others in life, and in death. No mean feat.

Professor David Cunningham, who cared for him at the Royal Marsden hospital, said in a speech at the post-funeral party that Philip had given strength to others to face cancer and to face death. He said he had never met anyone quite like him. Not a day has passed since that I have not felt intense sadness that he has gone, but intense happiness that I knew him so well when he was here, and that he went out in such style.

How much better to go like that than, as so many now do, unsure of who or where they are, or of who that person is crying at the bedside? I didn't like much that Margaret Thatcher did as prime minister, but hearing the stories of her friends and colleagues who met her recently, it was impossible not to feel real sadness. According to one of her closest friends, who sees her regularly, when she was wheeled out for a photo with Liam Fox, shortly before the Tory conference which was his last as Defence Secretary, 'she didn't have a clue who he was'. Covering her political demise was one of the happiest periods of my life as a political journalist, but I take no pleasure in thinking that a once sharp mind has been so badly numbed by illness. I have said to my kids that if I go doolally – again!! – and the option by then exists for euthanasia, I want to take it. The selfless reason is not being a burden. The selfish reason is that I want to die thinking my own happy thoughts about the life I have lived, about the family I leave behind, about a legacy of thought and action and experience. Death is bad enough any time. It is worse if the mind has gone.

As to whether Philip's death changed me, I couldn't see it at the time, but so many others have suggested that it has that perhaps he had a point. As the minister reminded the funeral service, 'poor Alastair' doesn't do God. Tony Blair was always convinced I would find God, but worried I would become an Islamic fundamentalist. Religious members of my family also think I will join them one day. So did Philip. Who knows?

It was certainly interesting to find priests writing to me after reading my eulogy in *The Times*, telling me they could sense a movement to God within what I said. Honestly! I also confess – no pun intended – to living through a series of remarkable coincidental and spiritual moments between Philip's death and the funeral.

I was constantly on the lookout for signs of comfort, not least to get me through reading out my letter the following Tuesday. One of my first public engagements after his death was handing out scrolls to graduates from South Staffs College in Lichfield Cathedral. Before the graduates arrived I asked if I could run through my speech for Tuesday. I thought it would help to do it in an empty church setting. It was hard. But as I looked up, the first thing I saw, above the altar, was a figurine playing the bagpipes. Why was that significant? Because I had also spoken at my father's funeral, and he was a piper. More, I was in the middle of making a film about the bagpipes for Sky Arts, and the next morning was flying to my dad's birthplace, the Isle of Tiree in the Hebrides, to meet up with relatives and play the pipes with my brother Donald. Then came another coincidence that also brought me comfort. The college principal, Graham Morley, was waiting for me as I finished reading. He had heard about Philip's death. He said he knew how I felt, as both his parents died from oesophageal cancer. Until Philip, I had never met anyone before who had died from this illness and now, as I rehearsed my tribute to him, I met a man who had lost both his parents to it. I don't know why but I emailed Philip's widow, Gail, and Fiona, to say for the first time I felt I might be able to get through Tuesday without cracking up.

There was more to come when I reached Tiree. After a day spent filming with aunts and cousins, and visiting haunts from my childhood, interspersed with playing the pipes, I slept badly. I got up at 6 a.m. and, in the dark, went for a run. I found my way, by accident, to my father's favourite beach. I ran on it, then stopped, fished out my BlackBerry and rehearsed my speech once more. Halfway through, tears streaming down my face, I noticed a solitary seal in front of me in the water. Philip, I thought. Then I noticed three more. Gail, and their daughters Georgia and Grace. Then I noticed five more swimming towards them. Me and my family. Then three birds flew by me, and swooped above the seals. Gail and the girls. It was breathtakingly beautiful. I looked up. The sun had risen.

I felt a happiness as intense as the sadness I felt at his loss. Both came together with a force I find hard to put in words. I still don't do God. But something pretty major was going on all around me.

I told Georgia the story. That night she had a dream in which her father appeared and told her everything was going to be all right. She woke up crying, failing to understand how he could be there in her dream, but gone from her life. She went for a run. She had her iPod on shuffle. The first song that came up was 'Three Little Birds' by Bob Marley, complete with the line 'Every little thing gonna be all right'. She called me to say we were both going to get through the funeral OK. We did.

Fiona and our children were the key to getting me through those days – my daughter Grace made me rehearse the most emotional bits again and again, in front of her, until I could do them without crying or my voice cracking – and enduring relationships are fundamental to the kind of happiness I am outlining. We row, we snarl, we hear but don't listen. But I'm happy we stayed together. When my first book came out Fiona was asked to write a piece on 'living with Alastair Campbell'. Like it was Aids or malaria. And this was her conclusion: 'On balance I am glad we stayed together.' Wow! Hardly 'I love him to bits'. Yet if we are being honest, such are the pressures put upon relationships – work, money, kids, all the stuff of marriage in a world where so many end prematurely – 'on balance I am glad we stayed together' is better than most long-term relationships can hope for. We've never married, but we're still very much together. Then of course there are three children. Everyone says they love their kids. Yet so many don't act in a loving way. It is hard bringing up kids. I read my diaries and the truth is I tried to devote any spare time to them. But I know it wasn't enough. Work–life balance is hard. It is hard for kids too. My daughter has just done her AS levels and is apparently part of THE most examined year in schools history. We should put our kids first but busy people can't and don't. But I am at my happiest when I am at my closest to them. I know this too – parents are never happier than their least happy child.

I am now at the age, fifty-four, when I do at least think about my own mortality. On the back nine of life as the golfer might say. I don't think I am alone in wondering what death will be like, wondering what my final thoughts will be, who will come to the funeral. I have a fair idea what the obituary writers are likely to say, because I am largely identified by my role with Tony Blair and always will be, though I hope between now and then to add to the obits in terms of experiences lived and contributions made.

On the final thoughts, I want to be able to say I had a full and fulfilling life because then I think I will die happy. So what will the components be? Family. Obviously you don't wish sadness upon those you love, but I want my partner and kids to love me, and to have felt I was good to them. I want to believe that when my dad died he considered me a good son, and that when my mum goes – she is into her eighties – she will think the same. I want to know I have enjoyed a good range of friendships, personal and professional. I want to know that some of my enmities were worthwhile, that I made life harder for people who deserved it – like Tories who think their divine right is to govern, or journalists who lie, cheat and never face up to the consequences of their lies and cheating.

I want to know I have worked hard and achieved much. I want to be able to say I was at least part of changing the world for the better, and whatever our critics say I know that the Labour government of 1997–2007 did plenty of that. I hope that by the time I die I will have played a part in ending the stigma and taboo surrounding mental illness. I want to write more books, see my first novel made into a film, fight more campaigns, work in more countries. I want to be able to recall experiences that have endured for their pleasure and range and intensity. And I know that at or close to the top of the list of best experiences of my life, one which helped shape the relative developing happiness I have, would be my nervous breakdown in 1986.

WHEN THE MIND CRACKS

My breakdown has given me a yardstick to use for the rest of my life, and against which to compare other bad experiences. It taught me what I thought and what I valued – family, politics, doing rather than just talking. It was also important because it gave me a taste of my own vulnerability and my own mortality. It was an irrational thought, but I seriously believed I was going to die. I was being tested – by what or by whom I didn't know – and

I was failing the test, and the punishment was going to be death. Unlike Philip Gould, I faced this fate with neither calm nor equanimity. I felt I hadn't lived long enough. I was scared of what lay beyond the last beat of the heart. The thought I was approaching it inspired more panic, which created more madness, greater certainty that death was a short distance away.

I was in a grey council building in the Scottish town of Hamilton. I had spent the day with the Labour leader Neil Kinnock for a profile I was writing for the *Today* newspaper. He was attending a dinner in the building. I was feeling odd, and looking for a phone to call Fiona. I found one in an office, and dialled home. No reply. Then my parents. No reply. Then Fiona's parents. No reply. Then I dialled any friend whose number I could remember. No reply from any of them. It was only later that I learned as soon as I had dialled the first digit – 0 – I was ringing an unmanned switchboard. It had not crossed my confused, panicking, crazy mind to dial 9 for an outside line.

I gave up on the phone and went in search of a quiet place to try to calm my mind, which now was racing but also being filled by noises that had never been there in such cacophony before. Music – bagpipes, brass bands, rock bands all clashing with each other. The voices of colleagues in the office shouting at each other. The voices of friends and family trying to calm me amid the noise, but failing to do so. I stood next to a lift. As people walked by, I assumed they were sending me messages whether they spoke or they didn't. I took their alarmed looks as further evidence that I was failing the test and being prepared for death. I had a shoulder bag with me. I emptied its contents onto the floor. I went through my pockets and did the same. I wouldn't need money where I was going, or a passport, or a notebook, or cigarettes, or a lighter. These all joined the little cairn of possessions on the floor. I haven't a clue what I was going to do next, and thankfully never found out. Two men approached me, who turned out to be Special Branch officers, asked if I was OK, and I said, 'No, I don't think so.'

It was the same week that Sweden's left-wing prime minister Olof Palme had been assassinated so the last thing they wanted close to Neil Kinnock was a deranged bloke in the foyer. They arrested me for my own safety. I was taken to Hamilton police station, put in a cell where I stripped naked, and began to scratch drawings on the walls. A kindly officer popped in to ask if I would like a drink of something … 'A bottle of your very best champagne please,' I said. He came back with a can of Irn-Bru. It was late, but eventually a doctor was found. Also Neil's press secretary Patricia Hewitt had realised I had gone missing, discovered what had happened and called to say there must have been a mistake. I was allowed to leave on condition I went to hospital. It was there that I finally faced up to a drink problem I had denied.

It was the hospital duty psychiatrist, Dr Bennie, who – without nagging – made me realise the years of denial had to end, and I had to accept I had a problem. A while after admission, he said he had noticed from my possessions – those I had put in the pile where the police picked me up – that I kept a diary. Did I record what I drank? he asked. I said no. But if I were to look at certain days, he suggested, would I remember roughly how much I drank? I think so, I said. He flicked through the pages and picked the day before my breakdown.

The day had started, as had many before it, waiting for Fiona to get up and go swimming, so that I could get up and go to the toilet to throw up last night's alcohol. Felt better. Into work. Wondering how early I could get to the pub. 11.20. Few pints. Back to work for a bit. Lunch with David Mellor, then a government minister. Three or four bottles of wine between us (I drank the bulk). Back to the office via a couple of quick ones at the Lord High Admiral. Leave jacket over chair and nip out after afternoon conference. Into double figures on beer, switch to spirits. Call home for a row with Fiona, who was angry because she'd made dinner and I wasn't home – again – and I was drunk – again. Ended up slamming down phone after saying I will go to a hotel not home. Well into double figures on spirits by closing time. To the hotel. Demolish minibar.

Now that was a particularly bad day but there had been others like it. As I looked at Dr Bennie, he had a little smile in his eyes. He knew that I knew. That in telling the story to him, I told it to myself, and the penny had finally dropped. It was a turning point in my life. When I met him years later, he said it was often the case that these revelations come suddenly like that. It's just that a lot of damage gets done while friends and family are waiting for the addict to face up to the truth.

But if I thought I might get the drink under control – I was dry for thirteen years and though I sometimes drink now I have not been drunk since

1986 – I was nevertheless convinced my career was over.

Richard Stott showed faith in me, however. He had been angry at my leaving the *Mirror* for *Today*. He had said I was not ready to be a news editor. He couldn't resist a little bit of 'I told you so', but he offered me a job back at the *Mirror* when I was fully recovered. I had to start at the bottom again, working night shifts and doing the rewrites of women's magazine interviews. I learned who real friends were and who the ones were who just wanted to get me back on the booze again. Slowly, I rediscovered something of my old passion for work. I realised too that politics was more important than I had let on to myself. Political journalism was where I wanted to be, and it is where I went. I loved it. I was only really beginning to tire of it when John Smith died, Tony Blair became leader of the Labour Party, and he asked me to work for him.

I took a month to decide. Fiona was opposed. My parents were opposed. Neil Kinnock was

opposed, and warned me it would ruin my life
and my family's life. But I felt it was a challenge I
could not duck. I had written hundreds of thousands of words about why we needed to get rid of
the Tories. Now I had the chance to help make it
happen. My own nagging doubt came from the
breakdown. I had cracked up before. I would come
under greater pressure doing the job Tony was
asking me to do than I ever did as a journalist. I
told him about it, in minute detail, one day on a
drive from Marseilles airport to the holiday home
where we were staying, and where he came to talk
me into working for him. He looked a bit alarmed
at times as I went through the whole story, but at
the end he said, 'I'm not bothered about any of that.'
I said, 'What if I'm bothered?' He said, 'I'm still
not bothered.' As the phone-hacking scandal has
unfolded, I've often wondered if David Cameron
and his ex-Director of Communications, Andy
Coulson, ever had that frank clear-out of skeletons
from the cupboard.

I have felt under huge pressure at times since. I have endured many frenzies and a few genuine full-blown crises. I have felt on edge. But I have never felt like I will fall over the edge. For that I thank my breakdown. So when I enter the death zone, I will give thanks for my family, Fiona and the kids especially. I will thank friends, dead and alive. I will thank the people who gave me all the amazing opportunities I have had to do things in work and play. But I will also have a little nod to my madness, vintage '86.

I don't thank my depression. I don't will it upon anyone. It is a horrible illness for which there is not enough understanding. The nearest I can come to describing it is that when it strikes you feel dead and alive at the same time. But I am content that I have learned to live with it; pleased that I have accepted it as part of who I am, happy that after years of living in denial finally I got help, and though I retain a lifelong abhorrence of drugs, pleased that I have a psychiatrist I trust enough to listen when he tells me: 'I think it might be a good idea if you took a few pills for a while.'

I'm happy that it inspired me to write my first novel, *All in the Mind*, about a psychiatrist and his relationship with his patients. As the novel unfolds it becomes clear he has problems every bit as serious as theirs, but no idea how to address them. The idea came to me while riding my bike. I became a man possessed until I finished it. I told nobody I was doing it until it was done. It was like an enormous force within me that had to come out. I was so happy when I wrote it, even though I cried a lot on the way, so happy when it was published, so happy at the letters I get from people who say 'I am glad I am not alone', just as happy that people write and say 'at last I understand depression a bit'. I want to feel I contributed to breaking down the last great taboo, so that people are as open about their mental health as they are about their physical health. We used to call cancer 'the big C'. Now we all know what to say when a friend or relative has cancer. As a society we have developed the language so that we can understand, support and sympathise. I want to do the same for schizophrenia, bipolar disorder and other mental illnesses.

That is about fulfilment; about taking the bad and turning it into something good, a more creative expression of an experience and a time when I thought I was going to die.

It is the same impulse – trying to get good from bad – that made me, on the basis of going for a rare run with my sons on holiday in France in 2002, decide there and then to enter the London Marathon 2003 and try to raise funds for research into the disease which killed John and Ellie. I entered the marathon, trained like a madman even though at the time we were in the middle of the run-up to the war in Iraq, and raised half a million pounds.

TEAMSHIP AND FRIENDSHIP
Sport is responsible for so much happiness and joy. If someone asked me to think of a week when I

was really happy – a whole week without a blemish – I might well go for the first Soccer Aid. I grew up wanting to be a footballer. The slight problem with that ambition was that I wasn't very good at it. Yet there I was, aged forty-nine, training under Ruud Gullit and Gus Poyet and ending up playing with four World Cup winners – Diego Maradona, Marcel Desailly, Dunga and Lothar Matthäus – in front of 72,000 people at Old Trafford, and millions more on TV. I came off and Rory said, 'Sorry, Dad, but you were so out of your depth.' 'I know. And I don't care. I loved every second of it.' I was happy.

I've often felt like a frustrated sportsman. My post-Downing Street life is almost as much about sport as politics. When I changed phones recently, in switching my contacts from one device to another, the shop assistant noticed I have more football managers than politicians in my address book. Inevitably, and as do so many others, I romanticise what it must be like to be at the top of football. Yet this world too has its share of suffering. The best book I read last year was *A Life Too Short* by Ronald Reng, the story of the German goalkeeper Robert Enke who took his own life after losing his battle with depression. To anyone wanting to understand the illness better, read it. And of course the world of football was shocked to its core recently when Wales manager Gary Speed, someone who was universally popular in the game, committed suicide. Problems of the mind are no respecters of wealth, race, profession or lifestyle.

But the sense of fulfilment that sport can generate runs deep. I cannot watch an Olympic ceremony without tears in my eyes. Often even the athlete isn't crying. But I see the flag, I hear the anthem and I cry with joy for that athlete and his or her fulfilment. I think of the thousands of hours they trained; the injuries; the sacrifice; the support of friends and family surely crying along back home. It can be a Bulgarian who got gold for Graeco-Roman wrestling, but it'll still set me off.

I learn so much from sport because I love building teams. I have been subject to a fair few political and media attacks in my time, but never by the people who worked directly for me. I would also say that the times when strategic communications played the biggest part in making change happen during the time I was with Tony Blair were not Iraq, despite all the controversy, but Ireland, Kosovo and the general election campaigns. In all, the satisfaction I felt was as a direct result not just of the outcomes, but the teamship required.

The next step up from teamship is friendship. Governments cannot create friends for you, but David Cameron was right to put the quality of relationships in his triptych. I know a lot of people. I get on with a lot of people. I don't have that many close friends. Not real friends that I know I could count on one hundred per cent. It doesn't help that several have died. Alex Ferguson, who I do count as a close friend, gave me the best definition of friendship I have ever heard: 'The true friend is the one who walks through the door as others are putting on their coats to leave.' I am happy with the friends I have. Some, like Alex, or Brendan Foster, or Tony Blair and other senior Labour figures, readers may have heard of. Others they won't know. But I think they would all walk through the door as others were putting on their coats to leave, and they know I would do the same for them.

Of the many things I have done since leaving Downing Street in 2003, one of the most interesting, and at times surreal, was when I was asked by Clive Woodward to manage the communications for the British and Irish Lions tour of New Zealand in 2005. It became clear fairly early on that the press were going to do their level best to make me an issue, and they did. It all got a bit irritating, and I was sounding off one day about how ridiculous they were, when the Lions chief executive John Feehan, a big bluff Irishman, said something wonderful in its clarity and simplicity: 'Ah, well, in the end all that counts in life is your friends and your family. If you've still got them, you'll not go far wrong.' He's not far wrong.

I've still got my mother. My father died after a long illness some years ago. The length of the illness did not prepare me for the shock or the impact when he died. I felt like I was living in a perpetual fog. I kept looking for him, and sometimes thought I could see him. We all know grief. So how can we still be happy, when we lose people we love? Only by learning from the experience, and living with what we have learned. Gordon Brown sent me a lovely letter when my father died, saying that every day he saw his own father standing in front of him, trying to give him guidance and strength. I try, and often succeed, to get similar strength and guidance from my own father, his ashes now scattered over the land where he worked as a vet. I wrote, and I heard, many sound bites during my time with Tony Blair. But as I said in my farewell letter to Philip Gould, the best of all I heard came not from me, or from any of the politicians or PR guys I worked with, but from the Queen, in the aftermath of the September 11 attacks more than a decade ago. 'Grief is the price we pay for love.' I was sitting near Bill Clinton. 'Did you write that?' he whispered. 'No,' I said. 'Well, find out who did and hire him.'

On the day I delivered the Happiness Lecture in Birmingham, I visited the haematology centre at the university and saw how £2.5 million of Leukaemia and Lymphoma Research money was being spent on clinical trials. I met patients, and not only were they alive, but in talking to them I felt the memory of John and Ellie was alive too. Trying to get good from bad. As a result of writing *All in the Mind*, and presenting an accompanying film about my own breakdown, I got involved with Mind, Rethink Mental Illness and the Time to Change campaign to break down the stigma and taboo surrounding mental illness. Trying to get good from bad.

So for me, happiness comes through fulfilment, personal, professional, political. I am an obsessive and a perfectionist and neither of these things are compatible with contentment, of self or of others. Yet I argue they are the traits that enabled me to do the job I did for Tony Blair, helping to win three elections and helping his government be a good one that made a lot of changes to Britain and the world. These days, politics plays a smaller but still significant part of my life. I make speeches. I write. I work as a consultant for governments, businesses, individuals, charities. I can get a five-figure fee for a speech to a conference or a board in the City. I'm not going to say no. But I get a lot more out of the unpaid pitch to M&S to persuade them to become a charity partner. Like the Canadian researcher who gave twenty dollars to people as a part of a study, measured their relative happiness a couple of days later, and discovered that those who spent the twenty dollars on someone else were happier than those who spent it on themselves.

So I have a family I love. I have a small number of close friends. I live in a friendly street. I support a football club and a political party and two charitable causes which all mean a lot to me. I have a complex sense of national identity – I am British first, then Scottish, then Yorkshire, then Londoner, then English, then European. All of these things make me connected. And the reason why money does not automatically make us happy is because it does not automatically connect us. If I had to list the countries where I sensed the most happiness, it would not be the UK, nor the US. It might be Australia. It might be Ireland, certainly before the crash. And it might also have been Ethiopia or Mozambique, because I visited places of extraordinary hardship yet where the sense of people as families and as communities was stronger than in the richer countries of the world. David Cameron should visit countries like this, not just to hand out development aid, as we should, but to learn what we lack from what they have.

I am lucky enough to have had two careers, and now a third, weird phase of my professional life, when for the first time since I became a journalist I have enormous freedom to do what I want to do, rather than what bosses want me to do. I will probably regret never standing for office myself, but other factors prevented me from doing so in the past, and I will be almost sixty when the next election comes. I get a lot of professional opportunities and I make a decent living. I am lucky enough also to give of my time and money to others – and survey after survey shows giving is as likely to make us happy as taking. So I feel happy enough with the life I have lived and the life I am living. But I won't know for sure until the day I die.

On that happy thought: keep smiling.

ENDNOTES

1   Cameron speaking at the Google Zeitgeist Europe
    Conference in 2006. Full text here: http://www.
    guardian.co.uk/politics/2006/may/22/conservatives.
    davidcameron

2   Ibid.

3   http://www.telegraph.co.uk/news/worldnews/europe/
    france/6189530/Nicolas-Sarkozy-wants-to-
    measure-economic-success-in-happiness.html

4   See Stiglitz and Sen's report on the Measurement
    of Economic Performance and Social Progress:
    http://www.stiglitz-sen-fitoussi.fr/documents/
    rapport_anglais.pdf

5   http://www.neweconomics.org/publications/
    national-accounts-wellbeing

6   http://www.cpag.org.uk/info/ChildWellbeingandChild-
    Poverty.pdf

7   http://www.telegraph.co.uk/news/uknews/1579887/
    Rowan-Williams-Children-are-too-materialistic.
    html

8   See Richard Layard's book *Happiness: Lessons From a
    New Science* (2nd edition, Penguin, 2011)

9 http://www.neweconomics.org/publications/
       national-accounts-wellbeing

10 http://en.wikipedia.org/wiki/
       Environmental_impact_statement

11 http://www.iim-edu.org/grossnationalhappiness/

12 'Psychologists have spent decades studying the relation
       between wealth and happiness, and they have
       generally concluded that wealth increases human
       happiness when it lifts people out of abject poverty
       and into the middle class but that it does little to
       increase happiness thereafter.' From *Stumbling On
       Happiness* (HarperCollins, 2006)

13 http://cep.lse.ac.uk/textonly/research/mentalhealth/
       DEPRESSION_REPORT_LAYARD.pdf

14 http://www.neweconomics.org/press-releases/nef-five-
       day-wellbeing-major-new-government-report

15 http://www.alastaircampbell.org/blog/2011/11/16/
       letter-to-a-friend-and-a-report-of-philip-goulds-
       funeral/

16 Serialised in five parts in *The Times* in July of 2011,
       Philip Gould described his battle with cancer in 'The
       Unfinished Life: An Odyssey of Love and Cancer'.

The first part is here: http://www.thetimes.co.uk/tto/
life/article3088455.ece

17 http://www.bbc.co.uk/news/uk-politics-14963442